# Reina visits the Butterfly Garden

Sheila C. Duperrier

# Reina visits the Butterfly Garden

By Sheila C. Duperrier
ReinaZone.com
*The zone for innovative kids and fun learning!*

Edition June 2022

Reina visits the Butterfly Garden
English (bg-EN)

While every precaution has been taken in the preparation of this book, the publisher assumes no responsibility for errors or omissions, or for damages resulting from the use of the information contained herein.

Copyright © 2022 Reinazone.com
All rights reserved.

Let's explore along with Reina all the beautiful things in the butterfly garden!

One day, Mom and Dad asked Reina to come to the butterfly garden. There she would have fun—that was for certain!

So they went to a place with so many flowers! Reina was happy and could be there for many, many hours!

She closed her eyes and breathed in deeply.
And all the flowers tickled her nose so very sweetly!

Everything was beautiful and bright.
The flowers were an incredible sight.

And so much to learn, so many butterflies to meet.
They flew in the air and landed at her feet.

When Reina was little she didn't like **bugs**.
She didn't like **spiders**, **flies**, and **slugs**.
But then she learned more
—and couldn't ignore

Here in the Butterfly Garden,
Reina met many butterflies.
She could hardly believe her eyes.
There were **Monarchs** and **Gray Hairstreaks**,
**Cloudless Sulphurs** and **Swallowtails**.

**Cassius Blues** and **Queens**—so many cool butterfly details!
So much to learn, so much to see;
this is exactly where Reina wanted to be!

She crossed fields of flowers so bright,
so many butterflies fluttering in the bright sunlight.

Reina laughed and waved to them as they flew; she even held out her hand for a **Cassius Blue**.

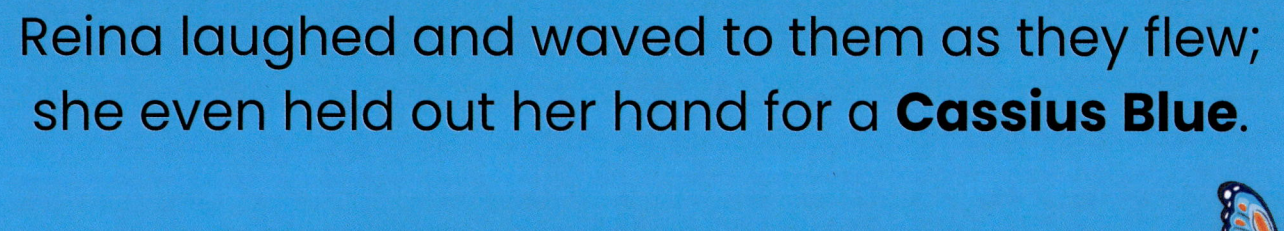

She learned butterflies can **taste** with their **feet**, and she thought that was really neat!

Like us, they can **drink** through their very own **straw**.
And that is what Reina saw.

Butterflies drinking **nectar** from flowers that day, and in such an exciting way!

She learned butterflies like warm, sunny places.
And everyone wore bright smiles on their happy faces.
Reina discovered butterflies **pollinate** plants,
helping them grow.
Oh, there was just so much to learn and know!

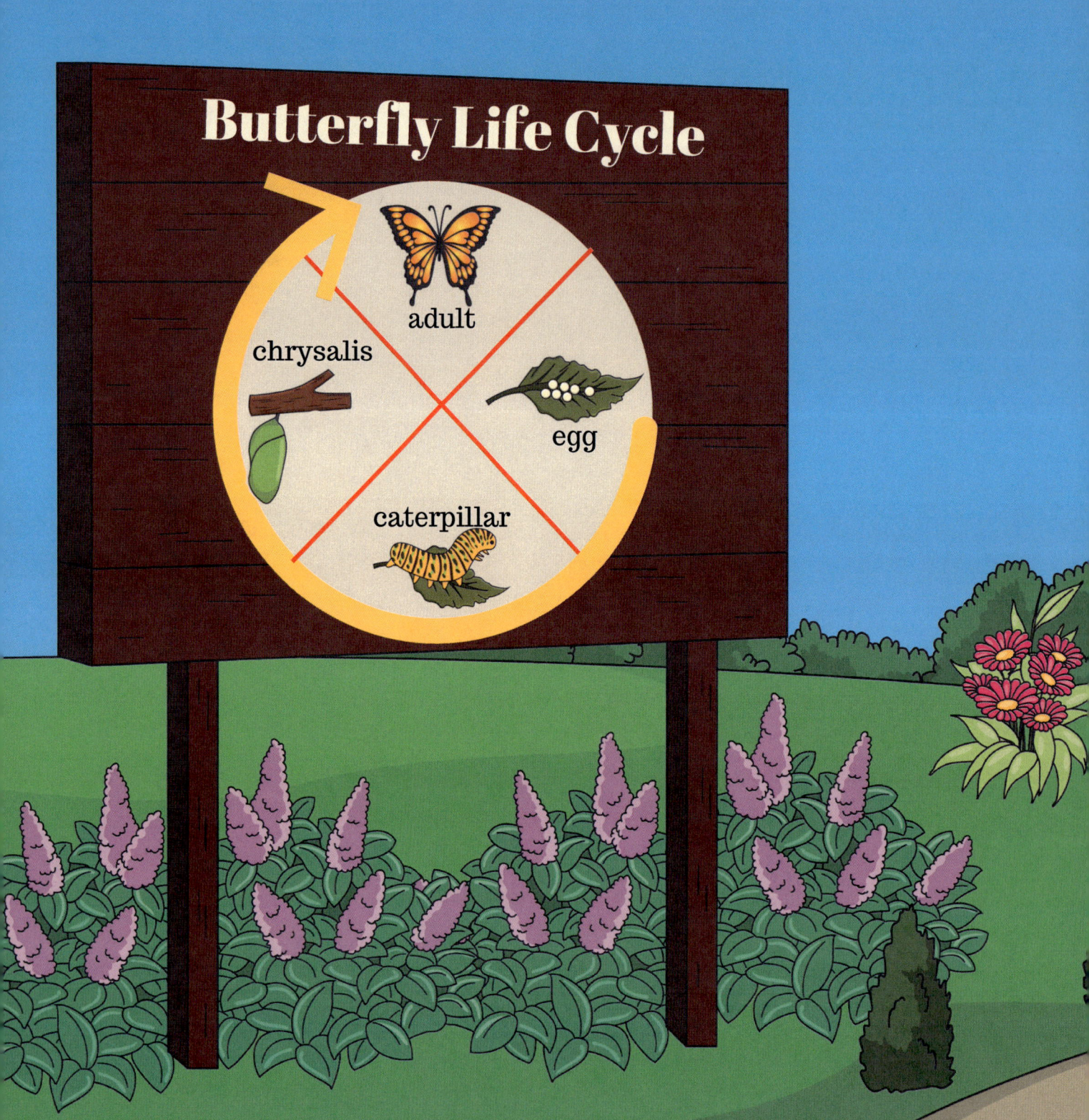

How do butterflies become butterflies?
Could they always fly?
Reina needed to know how and why.
Then she saw a big picture on display.
Showing butterflies growing in a wonderful way!

First, they are itty-bitty **eggs** so small!
Nothing more than a little ball.
Then they become **caterpillars**, crawling so slow.
But then what? Do you know?

They crawl onto a branch and make a **chrysalis** to sleep.
Shh, a deep, deep sleep.
They stay inside for 10-14 days, and then it is time to wake.
And what did this **caterpillar** make?

It is a butterfly, flying into the sky!
Reina waves to it as it flutters by.

She was so happy to be there and learn so much. It was so beautiful with butterflies to see and flowers to touch.

"Do you see?" said Reina. "All the wonders I've found?"
All her friends and family turned around.

"I didn't like butterflies and bugs before.
But today, I've learned so much more!
They're so pretty and sweet.
They're just the kind of bug I want to meet!"

Reina's little brother and friends had to agree. They loved all the butterflies on every flower and in every tree.

She had to go home, so she said goodbye.
And she would never forget each and every butterfly.

# Glossary

**Ant**: an insect that lives in large, organized groups called colonies. Most kinds of ants live in or on the ground. Ants are related to bees and wasps.

**Bee**: an insect with a hairy body, four wings, and sometimes a stinger. Some kinds of bees live in social groups, and some live alone. Many bees drink nectar from flowers.

**Bug**: any insect or crawling animal. Spiders and ants are often called bugs.

**Butterfly**: an insect with four large wings that flies mostly in the daytime. Butterflies are closely related to **moths** but have thinner bodies and are usually more brightly colored.

**Butterfly house** (also called a **lepidopterarium**): A conservatory or a facility that is specifically intended for the breeding and display of butterflies with an emphasis on education. See one on pages 6-7.

**Chrysalis**: the hard outside covering on a moth or butterfly while it is a pupa, the stage before it becomes an adult with wings. Many kinds of moths and butterflies make a chrysalis instead of a cocoon. Chrysalis is also sometimes used as another name for the **pupa** itself. See page 22.

**Caterpillar**: the **larva**, or second life stage, of a moth or butterfly. Caterpillars are round and long like worms but have 16 legs (6 true legs and 10 prolegs).

**Fly**: a fly is an insect with two wings. Most flies are active in the daytime, and many have large eyes. Mosquitoes and houseflies are among the thousands of types of flies.

# Words used in the butterfly garden

**Flutter:** to fly with quick, light wing movements.

**Insect**: a small animal whose body is divided into three parts (head, thorax, and abdomen). Insects also have three pairs of legs and usually one or two pairs of wings. Bees, ants, butterflies, beetles, and flies are kinds of insects.

**Larva**: an insect after it hatches from an egg and before it changes into its adult form. Larvae do not have wings and look like worms. Most kinds of insects spend part of their lives as larvae. **Caterpillars** are a type of larva.

**Moth**: an insect that has broad wings and flies mostly at night. Moths look like butterflies, but they usually have thicker bodies and bushy antennae and are less colorful.

**Pollinate**: to move or carry pollen to a plant, causing the seeds to be fertilized.

**Pupa:** (or chrysalis) an insect in the middle stage of its development, after it is a larva. Pupas do not eat or move; they are changing into their adult form. Many kinds of insects, including butterflies, spend their time as pupa inside a **cocoon**. See page 22.

**Spider**: a small animal with eight legs and a body made up of two parts. Most spiders spin webs in which they nest and catch insects to eat. Spiders are related to mites, ticks, and scorpions. See page 10.

**Slug**: a small land animal with a soft body and two tentacles with eyes. Slugs are mollusks closely related to snails, but they do not have a visible shell. They live in wet places and eat plants. See page 10.

**Author's note:**

Thank you very much for exploring the Butterfly Garden with Reina. If you enjoyed it, please consider leaving a review or recommending it to a friend.

To get the accompanying coloring book
Search for "Reina visits the Butterfly Garden – Activity book"
The activity book is packed with coloring pages, mazes, search words, dot-to-dot, facts, and much more to make your little one become a butterfly expert! **Get your copy today**.

Visit www.ReinaZone.com for more information.
Scan the QR code below to get your free gift now.
Thank you again for your support.

- **Sheila C. Duperrier**

Scan me

Made in the USA
Columbia, SC
21 November 2022